I Work at a Public Library

A Collection of Crazy Stories
— *from the Stacks* —

Gina Sheridan

Adams Media

New York   London   Toronto   Sydney   New Delhi

Adams Media
An Imprint of Simon & Schuster, Inc.
57 Littlefield Street
Avon, Massachusetts 02322
Copyright © 2014 by Gina Sheridan.

ADAMS MEDIA and colophon are trademarks of Simon and Schuster.

For information about special discounts for bulk purchases, please contact Simon &
Schuster Special Sales at 1-866-506-1949 or business@simonandschuster.com.

The Simon & Schuster Speakers Bureau can bring authors to your live event. For
more information or to book an event contact the Simon & Schuster Speakers Bureau
at 1-866-248-3049 or visit our website at www.simonspeakers.com.

Manufactured in the United States of America

10 9 8 7 6

Library of Congress Cataloging-in-Publication Data has been applied for.

ISBN 978-1-4405-7624-9
ISBN 978-1-4405-725-6 (ebook)

Dedication

For library users, workers, and lovers. And the #tumblarians.

Acknowledgments

A whole lot of thanks go to Kate McKean of Howard Morhaim Literary Agency; Tom Hardej and the team at Adams Media; Jayson Prouty and Sabrina Lunn, who helped immensely during the writing process; my friends at Fresno County Public Library and St. Louis County Library; and to Jeff Weddle and Martha Connor, my first and favorite librarian mentors.

To the many people who contribute their incredible library tales to the blog, especially the following individuals whose stories are included in this book: Carol Crosby Baker, Jen Bigheart, Andrew Bono, Nicole Brinkman, Kyle Brough, Barbara Conroy Flynn, Claire Gross, H. Susan Hackmann, Roma Havers, Anna Maria Huckeby, Shannon A. Jensen, Heather Johnson, Leslie Johnston, Vicky A. Klassen, Christina Martins, Jeremy Osgood, Hillary Rains, Maeve Rasmussen, Alexandra Raymond, W. Paul Rayner, Renata Sancken, Cady Steinberg, Kevin Toomey, Amy E. Volz, J. Waltmire, and Judith Wright.

To the readers, for there wouldn't be any blogs or books without you.

Finally, I'm especially grateful to Travis, who believed in this project before I did and was a constant source of energy, friendship, and encouragement. I love you!

Contents

Introduction

A Cold War spy in desperate search of Krispy Kreme dough-nuts, Cuckoo Carol dumpster diving for cans . . . again, and the inevitable fact that one day, somewhere, human excrement will end up on the floor. Maybe you expect these kinds of things to happen on, say, reality TV, but you never expect this to happen in your local library. However, as any public librarian will tell you, happen they do!

I didn't expect to write a book about the strangeness of everyday life in the public library. I went into library science with the expectation of quiet afternoons, challenging research questions, and the comforting smell of old books. But the day I discovered Cuckoo Carol digging around in the library's dumpster was the day I started collecting library stories. Expectation met reality in this one, unforgettable moment as I asked Carol what exactly she was hoping to accomplish in the dumpster. "I'm looking for aluminum cans! But I'm getting really thirsty. Just call me cuckoo!" Carol hollered from within. This was shortly after I started my first professional librarian position in California. New to town and new to Library Land, I had no idea that Carol was just one of a cast of colorful characters I would meet in my career. As I helped her step down out of the dumpster, I thought to myself: *I need to write this down!*

So it's because of Carol that I started writing and sharing stories, hilarious interactions, and crazy encounters on my Tumblr, *iworkatapubliclibrary.com*. To my surprise, people actually started reading and sharing the blog, and other library workers from around the world began to share their stories with me. The "I" in *I Work at a Public Library* quickly became a universal "I." I loved recording these stories and that other people, including many nonlibrary people, loved the sharing, insight, humor, and heart they provide.

In this book, you'll find some of the best stories, questions, and conversations that I have collected in my years as a librarian. The chapters that follow are categorized using that old library favorite—the Dewey Decimal System—turning this book into its own little library of sorts. The subject headings are like the ones you'd find in the stacks of your neighborhood library. From 004.16 Computers, stories of user error and technological flubs; to 598.2 Rare Birds, a whole chapter devoted to Cuckoo Carol; and ending with 809.9339 Volumes of Gratitude, a special collection of heartwarming tales of library (and patron) appreciation, *I Work at a Public Library* is for anyone who enjoys the absurdity and humanity of everyday life. All of these accounts are exactly as they happened at my own library or at a number of libraries from around the world. I offer them to you, objectively, without comment. Early on I received a note on my website from someone who said, "I had no idea the public library was so weird and wonderful." And that's exactly right.

Chapter 1

004.16 Computers

Humor is only a keystroke away at the library, especially in the computer lab when screening such questions as, "Am I allowed to view porn as long as it is sent directly to me?" or, "How do I copy and paste my dog's face onto my dad's in this photo?" The key to solving a patron's computer problem is to keep your hands behind your back while you are instructing the patron so she does all the clicking and learning, but also so you don't reach up and pull out your hair after the fifteenth right-click in a row. Take it from a librarian, a simple click is far from binding.

E-mail, Dirty Rotten

A woman waved me over to the computer she was using.

WOMAN: Yeah, how do I make it so my dumb ex-boyfriend can't e-mail me?

ME: I can help you with that. Are you signed in to your e-mail now?

WOMAN: I don't have an e-mail yet.

ME: You don't have an e-mail account?

WOMAN: Nope.

ME: Well, he can't e-mail you then. And if you do sign up for one, you don't have to give him the address.

WOMAN: That's good. That's how I want it! He's a scoundrel!

Rude, How

A woman approached the interior book return slot.

WOMAN: [*peering in*] Hello?

ME: Hi!

WOMAN: I was talking to the person at the other book drop but he was ignoring me, how rude!

ME: I'm so sorry, there is no one manning the outside book drop. Is there anything I can help you with?

WOMAN: Oh dear. Well, I was just asking him the difference between DVDs and CDs and could they all go in the same slot. Anyway, are DVDs those iPaddy things?

ME: Well, DVDs are movies. CDs are music or books to listen to. iPads are different.

WOMAN: How confusing! No wonder the fellow at the other book drop ignored me.

Face, About

A man came into the library to learn how to use the scanner.

ME: Let me show you. [*Walks him through the steps.*]

MAN: [*confused*] But how do I scan something other than a piece of paper?

ME: Like what?

MAN: [*Looking around, whispering.*] My face.

ME: —

MAN: It's for a dating site. This lady asked for a recent picture.

ME: Do you have a camera or a cell phone that takes pictures?

MAN: No.

ME: Wait here. I'll go get mine.

E-mail, Home

MAN: Yes, will these computers allow me to e-mail something to my house?

ME: Well, yes! The beauty of e-mail is you are able to open it from any computer with Internet access.

MAN: Well, I just need this specific e-mail to go to my house.

ME: I think I know what you mean. Let me show you. [*Signs him in and helps him bring up his e-mail account.*]

ME: See, if you just type your own e-mail address in, it's basically coming to *and* from you. In other words, there's a copy of your message in this account no matter which computer you use to open it.

MAN: So can I open it at home?

ME: Yes! Wait, you do have Internet access at home, right?

MAN: No.

ME: Oh . . . um . . . okay, I think I understand now. You kind of need the Internet to open it at home. How about we print your message out and you just take it home with you?

MAN: That's perfect.

Death, Screen of

GUY USING THE COMPUTER: I keep getting the blue screen of death.

ME: Sir, that's the desktop.

Lost, Get

ELDERLY PATRON: [*timidly*] Where are the computers?

ME: There are some in the Adult Department and in the coffee/vending machine area.

ELDERLY PATRON: Thank you. If I get lost, someone will come find me, right?

Internet, E-mailing the

PATRON: Is there a way to send a message out to everyone on the Internet?

ME: Yes, it's called a blog.

Not Firing, Hiring

A man called me over to help with the computer.

MAN: Can you help me with this job application?

ME: Sure. What's the problem?

MAN: Do you know if this is a good place to work? My friend says they're hiring, but do they fire people there?

ME: Well, probably.

MAN: Oh, never mind then. I don't wanna work there if they're gonna fire me.

Composers, We Are All

A man waved me over to the computer he was using.

MAN: Yeah, I'm inside my new e-mail address. How do I write a letter?

ME: Do you mean you'd like to write a message to someone? See this button that says "compose"? Go ahead and click on that.

MAN: Compose? Oh, okay. I thought that was for people who wanted to write songs. Composers, you know. It's amazing what you can do online these days!

Help, Needing

A man keeps wandering up to the desk to ask computer-related questions:

MAN: How do I make the computer like a typewriter?

MAN: There are red squiggly lines under everything I type. What do you suppose that means?

MAN: The computer keeps asking me to save my work to a disk and I'm not interested.

MAN: Now, eventually I want to make a website. Do I just get the framework up and going using the typewriter function? And do I just save it to a floppy to get it up on the website? And can I do any of this on one of your computers, or do I just take the disk home and do it there? Where is the Internet?

MAN: Maybe you could help me make a website. How long do you think it would take? I have about an hour.

Facebook, Working

PATRON: Hi there, doll, do you happen to know how to work Facebook?

ME: Yes, I do. What did you need help with?

PATRON: I need to find a Romanian woman I met last night. Her name is Ella and she was from out of town.

ME: Right, do you know her full name? Or where she is from?

PATRON: No, I just need you to bring up the full list of all the Ellas on Facebook.

ME: Sir, I think you might be underestimating how many people there are on Facebook and how popular a name like Ella is.

PATRON: Oh, okay, I'll just keep looking.

Rent, Won't Pay

I was walking by the public computers when a woman stopped me.

WOMAN: Can you help me? I need to make a ledger. I need to show what my renters have paid and what they owe me. And a column for late fees!

ME: Have you ever used a spreadsheet?

WOMAN: No. Can you just do it for me?

ME: I'm really sorry, but that will take some time and right now I'm in charge of helping people at the desk. You can make a one-on-one appointment with our computer instructor or take a computer class, if you'd like.

WOMAN: No, I don't have time for that. Can you just type me out a couple of letters then? These people won't pay rent!

Phone, Quacking

A man walked up to the desk with his smartphone in hand.

MAN: I can't make any sense of this.

ME: What are you having trouble with?

MAN: The volume. It keeps quacking instead of ringing. It's really embarrassing. I think my grandkids got hold of it.

ME: I think I can fix that. [*I take the phone, quickly go through the settings, and make a few changes. Then I show him the switch to quickly turn on and off the ringer.*]

MAN: You are a miracle worker! If only you could fix my grandkids. They could use an on/off switch. Or a kick.

Zoo, Petting

We were holding a Technology Petting Zoo in our meeting room so people could become acquainted with the various types of e-readers on the market. A young mother with a strange expression on her face poked her head into the room, so I asked if I could help her.

WOMAN: Oh, I'm really embarrassed. I thought it was a real petting zoo! Uh-oh, here comes my daughter. She'll be really upset!

DAUGHTER: [*A girl of about three who walks into the room, looks around, and quite dramatically says . . .*] Where are all the ponies? [*Begins to weep.*]

Favorites, Computer

A man using one of our public computers asked me for help.

MAN: Yeah, what's the difference between Microsoft Word, Google Chrome, and a website?

ME: Well, Word is a program you use to type something up, like a letter or a resume. Chrome is an Internet browser you'd use to look at websites. And a website is a space on the Internet to exchange information.

MAN: Which one do you like best?

United States, Google Versus

A man approached the checkout desk with a request.

MAN: I want to use one of your public computers, but could you please disable Google on it?

ME: Pardon?

MAN: I do not believe in, nor trust, Google. They are taking over the United States.

ME: I see. Well, I can't disable it, I'm sorry. But you don't have to visit the site if you don't want to.

MAN: That's not good enough.

ME: Come again?

MAN: I refuse to use the computers if Google is on them.

ME: Okay.

MAN: —

ME: —

MAN: —

ME: Enjoy your day!

Jobs, All the

I had a one-on-one computer appointment with a patron who needed help uploading his resume for a job application.

ME: You have your resume on your flash drive? That's great! Now which job are you applying for?

MAN: All of them.

ME: I'm sorry?

MAN: I'd like to apply for all the jobs on the Internet.

ME: [*gingerly*] Well, I'm sorry to say that's not how it works. I can show you how to upload your resume to a career site, but it's better to apply for individual jobs.

MAN: [*Holding up his flash drive.*] I can't just stick it in and let it go live?

Famous, I'll Be

A lady came into the library to ask for help transferring files from one flash drive to another.

WOMAN: Honey, I learned to back everything up. I dropped my old one in the dishwasher and I lost all the books I wrote!

WOMAN: [*Points to computer monitor.*] Remember these titles, darlin', because one day I'll be famous! You can say you knew me before I made it big.

- *Cabbage Patch Witches*
- *You and Me and General Lee*
- *Safety among the Rosebushes*
- *Learning to Let Go of Cheese*
- *The Vegan and the Carnivorous Carrot*

Chapter 2

025.52 Reference Work

You don't know if you don't ask. What better place to bring your inquiring minds than the place with the most massive wealth of knowledge in town? It's like the Internet, only the information isn't 90 percent false. Anyone can walk into the library and ask anything they please. And we will provide an answer. But when I think about my master of library and information science degree in relation to my average day at work, I have to laugh. Information science. I think about those two words when people approach the desk with questions like, "Where is the bathroom?" or "Can you open this tin of oysters?" or "Where can

I copy my face in private?" Information. Science. Peruse the following stories as a frame of reference, and keep in mind, common sense is often past due.

Questions, Fielding

While standing at the desk, you never know what crazy questions will come out of left field.

PATRON 1: Can you tell me what babies were born in Cleveland in June 1965? I think I am one of them! I just found out some stuff about my family.

PATRON 2: Where is the nearest waterfall? I want to dunk my head in it.

PATRON 3: Do you have a knife so I can cut this onion?

PATRON 4: What is the best way to cure hiccups, 'cause this kid is driving me nuts!

PATRON 5: What is the standard length of eyebrow hairs?

PATRON 6: Has my wife seen this movie?

Atheist, Suing an

PATRON: I need to know how to sue somebody. Can you tell me how to do that? And he's an atheist. Is that going to matter?

Help, Tax

A man approached the desk to ask about a tax form.

MAN: Is this the form I need if I'm a senior citizen and got a refund last year and itemize my deductions?

ME: Well, we can't help you decide which form to use, but I can look up the description of the form for you.

MAN: Just tell me if this is it.

ME: Let me read you the description—

MAN: Just tell me.

ME: I'm sorry, I can't. Let me read you the description.

MAN: Just tell me! Please.

At, Where I'm

Web chat exchange:

PATRON: I'm having trouble finding information through the library's website. Can you help me?

ME: Sure. Are you at the library's homepage now?

PATRON: No, I'm at my apartment.

Autobiographies, Dragon

I was helping a mother and her teenage son.

Mom: We need a book on dragons.

Me: I think most of those will be in the children's room, but let me check.

Mom: We want a biography of a dragon. No, an autobiography!

Satanism, Help with

A lady approached the desk to ask what kind of magical protection black salt would provide. Specifically, she wondered where she could get some and how she should use it.

Patron: [*very earnestly*] I don't care if it's Satanism, I need help!

Information, Contradictory

A well-known patron called the library:

Patron: Can you please help me? I am getting contradictory information—can you please tell me what today's date is?

Eunuchs, The Everything Guide to

PATRON: I am looking for a book on eunuchs, and it has to have lots of pictures, because that's the way I learn best.

ME: So you need a book with illustrations. Should this book explain the history or culture of eunuchs?

PATRON: Um, no. I need it to take me step by step through the process. And I need lots of pictures so I can follow along.

ME: So you need a manual? On eunuchs? Is there any particular stage of the process you are concentrating on?

PATRON: Well, I'm just starting out, just the basics of how it works. How to write the code, you know?

ME: Oh! You're looking for an illustrated manual for Unix!

Dislikes, Likes and

MAN: Can you give me a list of fun things to do in Seattle?

ME: I'm sure we could find you a travel book and get some ideas from their chamber of commerce!

MAN: That sounds good!

ME: Okay, what are some things you like to do?

MAN: Let me ask you this: What are some things *you* like to do?

ME: No, seriously—pick one: hiking, fishing, museums. . . .

MAN: But I really want to know what interests you. Come on, don't be shy!

ME: Are you going to Seattle, sir?

MAN: If I were, would you go with me?

ME: This is inappropriate.

MAN: I can't really afford it anyhow. Can you help me find a job?

Databases, Internet Versus

As a librarian, I help a lot of students with research. Often that means educating them on the difference between Internet resources and electronic databases. One day, I was showing a young man how to find good, quality articles using the library's online databases.

STUDENT: Oh, my teacher said I can't use the Internet.

ME: I'm sure he or she just meant you can't use Internet sources, but databases are different. You need the Internet to access them, but they are made up of encyclopedia articles and scholarly journals—

STUDENT: Yeah, I don't think that will work. Do you carry any books here?

Geography, United States

At my library in California, this surprising exchange occurred.

WOMAN: Do you have books on different countries?

ME: Yes! What country are you looking for?

WOMAN: Hawaii.

Meteorologist, Librarian as

It's been raining like crazy and a man just walked up to the desk to ask about the forecast.

ME: It looks like a flash flood warning is in effect for the metropolitan area until nine P.M. tonight.

MAN: Do you think it will stop raining anytime soon?

ME: Well, this report shows it will likely rain until midnight.

MAN: No, do you think it will stop raining soon?

ME: Me? I don't have any expertise with meteorology. We can only go by the weather report.

MAN: I'm asking for your opinion.

ME: —

MAN: [*staring at me*] —

ME: Um. Yes, I think it will stop raining soon.

MAN: Thanks! [*Walks away.*]

Chapter 3

028.9 Reading Interests and Habits

Erroneous book titles, strange recommendations, and countless opinions on reading material—the things patrons come up with can be pretty amazing. It's not uncommon for someone to come to the desk looking for "the book with the blue cover" or to tell us that someone has crossed out all of the curse words in the novel he just returned. "You must love to read" is the thing librarians hear the most, but really, we love to connect people with books. So if you need a book, or feel the need to physically alter one that belongs to the library, we've got you covered. Read on and become well-versed in reading interests and habits.

Confused, Thoreauly

A high school student asked if we had any books by Thor and Tyson.

ME: Sure! Are you looking for books on Thor, like the Thor from Norse mythology, and Tyson, as in Mike Tyson?

STUDENT: Um, I don't know. I need the books for class. [*Hands over a crumpled piece of paper.*] Here's what my teacher wrote on the whiteboard.

ME: [*looking at paper*] Oh, okay, you need books by Thoreau and Tennyson.

Books, Good

A woman came into our library, set a stack of movies on the counter, and loudly announced:

WOMAN: I have watched all your good movies. Do you have any good books here?

Books, Action

PATRON: Where are your books on action?

ME: By "action" do you mean like martial arts, that kind of thing?

PATRON: No, I mean like . . . [*mumbles*]

ME: I'm sorry, I didn't hear that, what did you mean?

PATRON: [*loudly*] Murder!

Fruity, Kinda

A woman walked up to the desk and asked for the book *The Grape Gatsby*.

WOMAN: They made a couple of movies, too. I don't know what it's about, but it sounds kinda fruity.

Irony, The Face of

A man with a blackened eye and a bandage over half of his face just returned a book. The title? *The Face of Battle* by John Keegan.

Biographies, Christian

PATRON: [*Gestures at son.*] He doesn't like to read, but he needs a biography. It has to be more than one hundred eighty pages.

ME: Do you know if autobiographies count? *Hole in My Life* is a pretty engaging story.

PATRON: What's it about?

ME: Well, Jack Gantos is a Newbery-winning children's author now, but when he was a teen he ended up in jail.

PATRON: [*Snatches book out of my hand.*] No. No. Absolutely not. I want something Christian.

ME: Well, uh . . . he learns a lot from being in jail and ends up being a writer who doesn't commit any more crimes.

PATRON: What about Anne Frank? Do you have anything about Anne Frank? He'd like that, right? It's got trapdoors and secret passages?

Titles, Questionable Book

What follows is a list of incorrect book titles library patrons have requested.

- *Catcher in the Wind*
- *Catch 22 in the Rye*
- *Dom Quicks-olay*
- *Gullible's Travels*
- *Fifty Shades of Grey's Anatomy*
- *How to Kill a Mockingbird*
- *The Girl with the Lizard Tattoo*
- *The Attic of Anne Frank*
- *The Diary of Aunt Frank*
- *Lord of the Flies by Tolkien*
- *The Hungry Games*
- *The Lively Bones*

Everything, Ruining

A disgruntled woman approached the desk.

WOMAN: I cannot *believe* the nerve of some people, dog-earing the pages of the books! Do they think they *own* the books? I think you should give a bookmark to every single person who checks out a book. I mean it. *They are ruining everything!* I will help make the bookmarks if that's what it takes.

Name, It's All in the

A patron approached the desk looking for an article for a class.

PATRON: I need the article "How to Talk about Sex" from *The Family Anal Editions.*

ME: [*Taken aback.*] You need what?

PATRON: [*Handing me her class syllabus.*] "How to Talk about Sex." It's from a publication called *The Family Anal Editions.*

ME: [*Looking at paper.*] Oh! You need *Annual Editions: The Family.* Annual. Not anal.

News, Good

PATRON: Can I get the newspaper?

ME: Yes, you can take this one right here if you want.

PATRON: Okay, but do you have other days?

ME: Oh sure, which date would you like?

PATRON: Do you know of a good one?

ME: Yesterday's was good.

PATRON: Okay, I'll take yesterday's.

Book, The Elusive

MAN: Do you guys ever have book sales?

ME: We have a standing sale. The table is right over there.

MAN: Oh, I've already looked over there. There's this book that I have been looking for for years. I can never find it at the library or garage sales or thrift stores.

ME: What is the title?

MAN: [*leering*] *Braille Sex.*

ME: —

MAN: —

ME: May I wait on someone else now?

MAN: I was just kidding.

It, Read

Patrons will often let us know when they really like, or hate, a book. One day, a woman expressed both emotions when returning two books.

WOMAN: [*Slams first book onto the counter.*] This book is born of the devil. It was absolutely repulsive and I don't think it would benefit anyone to read it. [*Lovingly places the second book in my hands.*] Now this one. This one, well, I insist that you read it. Insist! Do you think you could read it by next week? I'd like to discuss it with you. I bet you'll just love it. You'd better love it!

Experience, Firsthand

MAN: Do you have any books about how to become a prison guard? Specifically, how to become a prison guard if you've already had some experience as an inmate?

Books, Electronic

WOMAN: Yeah, I'm not interested in e-books. They will be the end of the library. Why would I want to help shut down the library?

ME: Actually, e-books are offered by the library, so we are happy when people check them out. We want people reading no matter what the format. Does that make sense?

WOMAN: But . . . aren't they invisible? I don't even know where they are.

ME: I can show you if you like.

WOMAN: I don't have time for invisible books when there are so many real books to read.

Table of Contents, DIY

MAN: This magazine's table of contents is on page twenty-five. Can you believe that? I should write in my own table of contents, including: *"too many ads, pages one to twenty-four."* That'd show them.

ME: —

MAN: Can I borrow a pen? Make it a marker.

Chapter 4

031.02 Curiosities and Wonders

Come one! Come all! Bearded ladies? Got 'em. Public bodily excretions of all kinds? Yep. The circus only comes to town once a year, but the library is always there to amaze and entertain. Witness the sights, smells, and sounds of awe-inspiring animals, lively characters, and feats of marvel. The best part? Admission is free. Ladies and gentlemen, boys and girls, keep your hands and feet inside at all times and behold the curiosities and wonders of the public library!

Dog, Service

I noticed a woman carrying around a shih tzu in the library.

ME: I'm really sorry, but we only allow service animals inside the library. People could be scared or allergic.

WOMAN: But look how cute!

ME: She sure is! But remember for next time, okay? It's our policy.

WOMAN: But . . . but . . . she's a service dog.

ME: [*unconvinced*] Oh?

WOMAN: Her service is being cute! [*Lifts the dog up and kisses it on the lips.*]

Cats, Library

First thing one morning, a man came up to the desk to ask if we had a library cat.

ME: You mean a cat that lives here? Sadly, no.

MAN: I just read a book about a library cat. I think this library should get a cat!

ME: I don't think it's in the cards. But that would be neat, huh?

MAN: Tell you what. I'll donate a cat. I'm sure there are some free kittens listed on Craigslist.

ME: Please don't do that. We love animals, but we can't have a library cat.

MAN: How about a puppy?

Everything, Location Is

A hyperactive man in the reading room approached me.

MAN: Hey buddy! Hey buddy, do you work here?

ME: Yes, may I help you?

MAN: Yes. Where's the library?

ME: This is the library. You're standing in it.

MAN: Oh, thanks, man!

Hurry, In a

A man was anxiously waiting for our fifteen-minute express computer to become available.

ME: Sir, there are some other computers open—would you like to use one?

MAN: No thanks, I'm in a hurry and I need an express one.

Donation, Library

On the floor of the lobby I found a plastic grocery bag containing two packages of uncooked chicken. Just outside the door was a man with a similar bag.

ME: Sir, is that your bag in the lobby?

MAN: [*in broken English*] I put bag there, but it is not for me.

ME: So, is it trash?

MAN: No it is not trash. It is donation.

ME: Uh . . .

MAN: I went to store, bought too much. The rest is for you. You can have it, madam.

ME: —

Beer, Flushing the

MAN: Them's toilet is broke.

ME: Pardon me?

MAN: Yer toil*ette* . . . it's broke.

ME: Oh! Is it not flushing? Did it overflow or . . . ?

MAN: It 'pears someone put a Pabst down that thang.

ME: Beer?

MAN: Yar. A can of it.

ME: I'll go check it out.

MAN: Waste of a beer, y'ask me.

ME: Yessir.

Case, Just in

A man asked me to look up an address for him. When I found it online, I offered to print it out but he declined.

MAN: I'll just write it down. Do you have a pencil?

ME: [*Hands him a pencil and piece of scrap paper.*]

MAN: [*Writes address down, then flips the paper over.*] I'm going to write it here, too, so I have a backup.

Birthday, It's My

I happened to be in the lobby when a pink-haired woman walked in the front door, ripped some library event flyers down from our bulletin board, and threw them in the recycle bin.

ME: [*calmly*] Why did you do that?

WOMAN: I was heppin' you out. And it's my birthday, so get out of my way. [*Exits the library.*]

Sale Books, Checking Out the

A woman approached the checkout desk with three books she'd previously purchased from our book sale.

WOMAN: Yes, may I return these?

ME: What? No. Why?

WOMAN: Well, I'm done with them now. If you can't give me my money back, can I go trade them for three more sale books?

ME: What? No. That's not the way it works. That is the way library books work, however. Why don't you check some of those books out and return them when you're done? Then you can get some more.

WOMAN: Oh, okay.

Margaritas, Library

A sweaty patron walked up to the desk on a very hot day.

PATRON: Where is the margarita machine?

ME: [*chuckles*] That's funny; it is hot out there.

PATRON: [*Stares at me with a straight face.*]

ME: Oh, did you think we had margaritas? Did someone say we had margaritas?!

PATRON: [*Keeps staring.*]

ME: I'm sorry. We don't serve margaritas at the library.

PATRON: [*Turns around and walks away.*]

Cover, Blown

PATRON: [*Pointing to my city employee lanyard.*] Wow, that's cool. How do I get one of those?

ME: You have to work for the city.

PATRON: I do! I'm an undercover police officer.

ME: Well, in that case, you probably don't want to call attention to it.

PATRON: [*After a bit of a pause.*] You're very smart.

Cycling, Library

I once came across a man riding his bicycle through the library. When I approached him he said he didn't want to leave it outside because it was raining and he didn't have a lock.

ME: I can understand that, but sir, you can't ride through the library.

MAN: It's not like I'm on a motorcycle, lady! [*Rolls out of the library.*]

Spine, Broken

WOMAN: [*pleasantly*] I'm bringing back this book, but I wanted you to know that the spine is broken. It wasn't my fault!

ME: No problem, it happens all the time in libraries. I'll take care of it.

WOMAN: But I shouldn't be charged for it.

ME: Right, you won't be. Like I said, it happens a lot. Thanks for letting us know.

WOMAN: It's because I'm honest. I honestly didn't do it. You don't know me, but I've never told a lie.

ME: That's great! I'm glad.

WOMAN: [*angrily*] Who are you, anyway? I've never seen you here before.

Time, Voting

A man approached the information desk.

MAN: Yeah, is it voting?

ME: I'm sorry?

MAN: Is it voting time?

ME: Tomorrow is Election Day.

MAN: Oh, okay, cool.

DVDs, Too Many

A man came to the desk with a stack of DVDs in his hands.

MAN: I don't think you should carry so many DVDs in a library. More books would be better.

ME: Well, we offer many different things for many different people. Would you like me to put those away for you?

MAN: No, I'd like to check them out.

December, When Is

A patron came in to the library to renew some overdue items.

PATRON: Do I have to pay the late fines?

ME: Yes, the items were late, so you have some fines.

PATRON: Oh, well I didn't know when December started and you guys didn't tell me.

Chapter 5

153.733 Listening In

They say that in space no one can hear you scream. In a library? Not so much. That said, shushing is such an antiquated, clichéd idea. In most modern public libraries, staff and patrons are expected to speak in normal indoor voices (granted, "indoor voice" is a relative term). It's quite hard to block out the bits of juicy conversation overheard in the stacks or ignore the serendipitous sounds that float through the book return slot. Each of the following entries are things overheard in the library. With so many thoughts and opinions at work, there is no better place to keep your ears open.

Envy, Library

Four-year-old girl upon entering the library and viewing the arches and columns in our main foyer:

GIRL: I am in a *castle!*

Calling, Name (Redux)

ME: You have an overdue item.

PATRON: What is it?

ME: *Charlotte's Web.*

PATRON: [*Turning to seven-year-old daughter.*] You turd.

Video Store, The Library as

I overheard a young woman showing her mother how to search for items in the library's online catalog.

MOTHER: There are almost three thousand movies to choose from?

DAUGHTER: Well, movies and TV shows.

MOTHER: There are TV shows at the library? Who would get those?

DAUGHTER: Lots of people.

MOTHER: So are you saying that the library is now the video store?

DAUGHTER: Among other things.

MOTHER: Who else knows about this?!

Snapshot, Library

The following is a conversation I overheard between a librarian and a coworker.

LIBRARIAN: Did you hear that that lady Sheila freaked out at our public printer yesterday?

COWORKER: Who's Sheila? Is she the one whose husband peed on the chair?

LIBRARIAN: No, she's the one who got into a fight with that lady Mary one time. You know, Mary is the one who puts up all the mirrors around the study carrel so she can see if anyone is spying on her.

COWORKER: Oh, I know Sheila. She's the one who wanted to use our meeting room to hold church services for magicians.

LIBRARIAN: No, no, that's Debbie. She also got into a fight with Mary though. Sheila is the one with the throat tic who doesn't ever use Print Preview.

COWORKER: Aw, man, I know that lady. . . .

Facebook, The

Comment from a seventy-year-old man to his wife:

MAN: I think we really should do the Facebook. Art and Frieda are doing it. We don't want to be the only ones left.

Fashion, Horror

I cohosted a teen trivia contest at the library.

ME: R.L. Stine is one of the world's most prolific horror writers for young adults. What do the initials in his pen name stand for?

TEEN: [*Without missing a beat.*] Ralph Lauren. [*Fist pumps.*]

Screwed, Completely

WOMAN AT REFERENCE DESK: I want a book but I only know the title. Am I completely screwed or what?

Assignments, Bombing

I found this exchange in our web chat archive:

PATRON: I would like information about the bombing of the internment camps, please.

LIBRARIAN: Do you mean you want info about the Pearl Harbor bombing? And then some information about Japanese-American internment camps?

PATRON: Oh! Now it makes sense!

Pizza, Stupid

Snippet of conversation I overheard while passing through the computer lab:

MAN: Do you want to get a pizza?

WOMAN: That is the stupidest thing I have ever heard you say.

Question, Good

As I was walking through the children's room, I overheard this exchange between a small boy and his mother:

BOY: Mommy, have you ever wondered what the inside of my eyelids look like?

MOTHER: I've got my own eyelids to worry about.

Fairies, Book

As I shelved books in the children's area, I overheard two parents talking as their children played.

PARENT 1: Do you ever hide books you've read over and over again because you're so sick of them?

PARENT 2: Oh, definitely. When they ask for them, I say the book fairy came to get it. One time they saw one of the books at the library so now they think the librarians are book fairies.

Library, Locked in the

This exchange occurred between two colleagues at a staff meeting:

LIBRARIAN 1: Oops. I just found out we locked someone in the library the other night. I'm glad it wasn't my night to close!

LIBRARIAN 2: That was like my secret dream when I was a kid. It's probably not as fun as I thought it would be.

LIBRARIAN 1: Especially for this poor lady—she was locked in the lobby. Nothing there but tax forms!

Found, Lost and

PATRON: Did anyone turn in a wetsuit?

Hard, Change Is

A regular patron approached the librarian who was helping out at our branch.

PATRON: Pardon me, but could you check this in for me? I'd like a receipt. Also, could you get someone else to help me? I've never seen you here before. Thanks.

Chapter 6

302.2 Communication, Failures and Disruptions of

The truth is out there, but the truth also seems to be very subjective. With access to so many types of information, there is bound to be some miscommunication that goes on in libraries. "Some" could be an understatement. Okay, there is *a lot* of miscommunication happening. To combat this, librarians strive to develop excellent listening skills, impeccable library instruction, and good follow-up questions. And a killer poker face hidden by a fashionable pair of glasses never hurts. Read on for the best and worst of miscommunication at the library.

Whiffy, Getting

A regular patron approached the desk.

WOMAN: Excuse me, what is "whiffy"?

ME: Pardon?

WOMAN: Whiffy. On your front door it says "Free Whiffy."

ME: Oh! WiFi. It's wireless Internet. So you can connect your device to the Internet.

WOMAN: So how can I get it?

ME: Well, do you have a tablet or smartphone or . . . ?

WOMAN: No. Do I need something?

ME: Yes.

WOMAN: Oh, ha! Never mind!

W, A Through

I was at the checkout desk when two incredibly drunk men approached.

MAN 1: We'd like to reserve all the movies A through W.

ME: Well, that's not really how it works. You can make a list of movies you want and we can order them for you.

MAN 2: Yeah, okay. A through W.

ME: That's not a thing.

Number, Personal Identification

A man walked up to the desk to ask what the PIN associated with his library account was.

ME: It looks like your PIN is twelve seventeen.

MAN: [*Looking utterly confused.*] I have no idea why I would've chosen that. Can you change it to one two one seven?

Vocabularies, Sluggish

A man came into the library to look for some cookbooks.

MAN: I'd like something that pays attention to what kind of vocabulary you have. I've been told mine is sluggish.

ME: Vocabulary?

MAN: I mean metabolism!

ME: Oh, ha, okay. Let me see what we have. [*Looks at catalog.*]

MAN: Yeah, you know how some people have fast vocabularies—

ME: —metabolism!

MAN: —and some people have slow ones . . . I guess mine is slow.

ME: Right.

Library, Cursing in the

MAN: How do you spell "curse"?

ME: C-U-R-S-E.

MAN: That can't be right.

ME: Curse? Like putting a curse on someone?

MAN: No! See, I knew you had it wrong. I mean like curse words.

ME: Oh! It's actually the same spelling, C-U-R-S-E.

MAN: Maybe I'll just look it up. . . .

ME: Well, okay, but that's how you spell it.

MAN: Oh, I believe you. I just want to look at other words like it. Like the adverb or adjective for it.

ME: —

Selfie, What Is a

A man walked up to the reference desk.

MAN: I have a question. What is this "selfie" thing everyone is talking about on the Internet?

ME: A selfie is slang for a picture you took of yourself.

MAN: Oh, that makes so much sense now. Also, what is . . . [*Looks at a piece of paper.*] S-T-F-U?

ME: Let me show you how to look these things up.

MAN: That'd be great.

TV Producer, The Library as

MAN: [*Holding up a DVD set.*] I really hope you get more seasons of The Wire in.

ME: We can request whichever season you need if we don't have it on the shelf. Which one are you missing?

MAN: Well, I've seen all five seasons, I just hope you get more.

ME: You mean you hope they make more episodes?

MAN: Yes, that's a great idea!

ME: —

Library, Just the

A petite elderly woman using a walker came into the library. From her position by the front entry, she hollered:

WOMAN: ISN'T THERE A COMPUTER CLUB MEETING TONIGHT?

All of us at the desk sort of looked at one another in wonder at this tiny woman. Such a powerful voice she had!

WOMAN: HELLO? IS THERE A CLUB MEETING TONIGHT?

ME: [*Quickly swooping in next to her.*] Hi there. What's the name of the club? I can check our meeting room calendar.

WOMAN: OH, PHOOEY. I DON'T KNOW. I JUST KNOW THEY USUALLY MEET THE FIRST MONDAY OF THE MONTH. THIS IS THE COMMUNITY CENTER, RIGHT?

ME: I'm sorry, it's not. It's the library.

WOMAN: WHAT?

ME: THE LIBRARY. IT'S JUST THE LIBRARY. I'M SO SORRY!

Audiobooks, Watching

As I was shelving some audiobooks, a woman approached me.

WOMAN: Are those books on DVD?

ME: Sort of . . . they're books on CD.

WOMAN: So, you can watch them?

ME: No, see, it's a recording of someone reading the entire book. You can listen to it on a CD player, like in your car or on a computer.

WOMAN: [*turning away*] Oh, I'll just wait till the movie comes out.

Earl, Hail to the

PATRON: I need to know the earl for the county?

ME: The earl? What do you mean?

PATRON: You know, like the website.

ME: You mean the U-R-L?

PATRON: Oh, is that how you say it?

Friends, Finding

WOMAN: Can you show me how to use Adult Friend Finder?

ME: Pardon?

WOMAN: Adult Friend Finder. I think it's a great idea.

ME: [*Knowing it's an adult hook-up site.*] Um, okay, we might have to override the Internet filter. Let's see. . . .

WOMAN: Wait, what?

ME: [*discreetly*] Because it might be in the pornography category.

WOMAN: Wait, what? I just wanted to make some girlfriends to go shopping with and stuff! I'm new to town. You know how hard it is to make good friends as adults? I thought it was just a friend site.

ME: No, huh-uh.

WOMAN: [*crestfallen*] Oh.

ME: You could come to some library events. You might meet some friends that way. . . .

Better, Feel

PATRON: I hope you feel better soon!

ME: [*confused*] I'm sorry?

PATRON: You have green nail polish on.

Holidays, Mixed-Up

MAN: When did Mother's Day become a federal holiday?

ME: [*looking up, confused*] Wait. . . . What?

MAN: Your sign here says you'll be closed on Mother's Day.

ME: Oh, no, the sign says that we are closed for Memorial Day.

MAN: Maybe they're the same day this year?

ME: Umm, no. Mother's Day is always a Sunday and Memorial Day is always a Monday.

MAN: I guess I read it wrong.

ME: Yes, I think so.

Class, The Case of the Mysterious

A woman approached the desk with the book she'd placed on hold.

WOMAN: Yes, I'd like to check this out for the duration?

ME: Pardon me? The duration of . . . ?

WOMAN: My class?

ME: Oh, okay. Well, you can check items out for up to eight weeks if no one is in line.

WOMAN: They told me I could have it!

ME: I'm sorry? Who told you, huh?

WOMAN: It's for my class.

ME: —

WOMAN: —

ME: How long do you need it?

WOMAN: I'm not sure when the class ends.

ME: I don't know what to say.

Merchandise, Library

MAN: Do you have any library merch?

ME: You mean like this book bag we have for sale?

MAN: No, I mean like books.

ME: I'm sorry, I don't understand what you mean.

MAN: Do you have books here?

ME: [*Opens arms in the direction of the stacks.*] Yes.

MAN: Thanks, I'll look around!

Yourself, Help

PATRON: [*Points at slip of paper.*] I want this title for my grandson.

ME: [*Looks it up.*] It looks like a self-help book. Does that sound right?

PATRON: What's self-help?

Chapter 7

302.343 Bullying

This isn't the schoolyard, so we don't expect someone to suddenly yell, "*Fight!*" And more often than not, your lunch money is safe and wedgies are pretty rare. But the truth is, there is no escaping it: Bullying happens everywhere, even the library. Bullies like to complain, ask questions to which there are no right answers, point out perceived injustices, slam their books down on the counter, and otherwise behave like twits. When it comes to dealing with them, the trick is to be patient, firm, and overly kind in order to keep your blood pressure down and the situation from escalating. If you are a library worker, take a deep breath before you read the following stories, and if you're a patron, well, don't act like these people or we'll throw the book at you.

Lip, Expecting

A man asked to speak with the person in charge.

ME: How can I help you, sir?

MAN: I'm a taxpayer and your door is broken and all of my money is going right out the door with the air conditioning!

ME: [*pleasantly*] Oh my! Let's go take a look. [*Walks to vestibule, adjusts button on automatic door.*] There we go. All better. It looks like someone bumped into it maybe.

MAN: You fixed it?

ME: Yes.

MAN: Well, I'm glad I said something. Most people wouldn't say anything, you know. I was going to write to my congressman if you gave me any lip, but you are very nice.

ME: Yes! Thanks. Bye!

Up, Dressed

As I was walking by the computer area around closing time, one of our more complicated regulars stopped to "compliment" me.

WOMAN: [*with perturbed tone*] Well! You look nice. It must be dress-up night at the library. You're in a prom dress and here I am in my ratty old T-shirt, thanks a lot! I'm only kidding. But you do look nice. Your complexion is much better these days, too. You must be drinking enough water. Well, goodbye.

ME: Thanks very much, bye. [*Looks in befuddlement at "prom dress," a cardigan over a black dress.*]

Disease, Cataloging

I was organizing the board games in preparation to catalog them, when a patron asked what I was doing.

ME: Well, I don't like the game pieces floating all over the place in the boxes, so I'm putting them in little baggies.

PATRON: [*with a serious tone*] Your obsession with organization is probably due to the fact that you have some psychological disorder that could easily be cured with antidepressants. I can recommend a great psychiatrist, if you'd like.

Out, Figuring It

ME: That'll be eighty cents for the eight copies, please.

MAN: Here's one dollar.

ME: [*Gives him two dimes change.*]

MAN: And here's a nickel.

ME: [*Looks at the nickel.*]

MAN: [*smugly*] Let's see how long it takes you to figure it out.

ME: So you want a quarter?

MAN: [*with a smirk*] Bravo!

MAN: [*One minute later.*] Hey, there's a paper jam!

ME: You know what I could say to you now, right? But I'm too polite.

MAN: Touché.

In, Letting Them

Note found in the patron suggestion box:
"You have SIGNS up near the computers that say BE QUIET, but people don't be quiet. They laugh out loud and talk out loud. Libraries used to be quiet, but they aren't anymore because you let all the *assholes* in!!!!!"

Day, Cold Winter

On a particularly cold winter day, a patron in the reference room approached me.

PATRON: "It's *too cold* in here. What is wrong with you people? Do you like frozen books?!"

Tax Forms, Hidden

MAN: Where are you hiding the tax forms?

ME: They're right over here! Let me walk you over.

MAN: Last time they were out in the lobby.

ME: Last year? Oh, well, this year they are over here.

MAN: I don't know why things always have to change.

ME: I know what you mean. Is there anything else I can do for you?

MAN: Move them back.

ME: Well, have a good day.

Taxpayer, But I'm a

WOMAN: There is no way I'm paying my late fee; I'm a taxpayer.

ME: [*Scanning her card.*] Let's take a look at your account, okay? All right, it looks like you returned one book one day late, so you owe twenty-five cents.

WOMAN: But I'm a taxpayer, and I'm pretty sure I've paid more than twenty-five cents to the library.

ME: No disrespect, ma'am, but everyone who has a library card is a taxpayer. Look, you don't have to pay it today if you don't want to.

WOMAN: I'll never pay it.

ME: Okay, bye-bye. Thanks for coming in.

Teen Section, The

One day, I overheard an adult male patron talking to his friend as they walked through the library.

MAN: This is the teen section. It's basically a bunch of dumb girly vampire stuff.

TEEN GIRL: [*Looks up while doing homework.*] Haven't you read John Green? Or Markus Zusak? They are incredible authors.

ME: [*to teen*] Those are a couple of my favorites. You have great taste.

MAN'S FRIEND: [*to all of us*] I've read all of John Green's books and seen all of his online videos. He's hilarious. [*to his friend*] Do you even read books?

MAN: —

Walking, No Fat People

I was working at the reference desk when a man approached from the direction of the computer lab.

MAN: Can you make it so fat people don't walk up and down the aisle of the lab? The floor shakes in a most distracting way.

Computers, No

A woman who was quite upset approached me at the desk.

WOMAN: When did you go and get rid of the card catalogs? How am I supposed to find anything in this labyrinth?

ME: Well, we created a computerized system many years ago now. May I show you how to use it?

WOMAN: No! No computers. I want you to tell me where a book is. *Without using the computer!*

ME: —

WOMAN: —

ME: —

WOMAN: I just want a book.

Place, Wrong

I was working in the children's library when a woman came up to the desk, shaking a figure-drawing book in her fist.

WOMAN: I can't believe you would shelve this in the children's area!

ME: [*Looking over the book.*] This is an adult book. You're right; it doesn't belong over here. Where did you find it?

WOMAN: On top of the shelf. I'm furious!

ME: I'm very sorry. I'll make sure it gets shelved in the correct place. Sometimes people leave things in the wrong place. I think that's what happened.

WOMAN: I could have you fired, you know.

Books, Banned

I was putting up a display for Banned Books Week when a mother and her six-year-old daughter stopped to watch.

GIRL: What're you doing?

ME: I'm making a display about books that people complained about. They wanted them removed from the library.

GIRL: Why?

ME: Because they didn't like what the books were about and didn't want anyone else to read them, either.

GIRL: I don't get it.

ME: I don't, either. Can you imagine what would happen if every person could choose one book to remove from the library forever?

GIRL: [*Quietly, with realization.*] There wouldn't be any books left on the shelves.

ME: That's right! It wouldn't really look like a library anymore, would it?

GIRL: We are learning about bullying at school. It sounds like even libraries get bullied sometimes.

ME: You are very smart.

Calling, Name

One evening, it was proving to be quite difficult to get a few of the patrons heading toward the door at closing time.

ME: Ma'am, is there anything else we can help you with today? We are about ready to close up but we'll reopen tomorrow at nine A.M.

WOMAN: You are a book nazi!

ME: A book nazi?

WOMAN: That's right. [*Throws up her hands and walks out.*]

Disgust, Anger and

A woman came to the desk with a look of anger on her face.

WOMAN: You hardly have *any* sale books over there. What the *hell* am I supposed to do?

ME: [*smiling*] I'm so sorry we don't have a lot of sale books right now. We do have many, many, many free books. [*Gestures at the stacks.*]

WOMAN: [*angrily*] Ugh!

Chapter 8

598.2 Rare Birds

Carol—a fiery, fierce, dumpster-diving lady—
dubbed herself "Cuckoo" shortly after our first
encounter at the library. She was my favorite
patron—don't worry, I changed jobs, Cuckoo
Carol is still alive and kicking—and the whole
reason I wanted to record library stories in the
first place. Her adamancy, eccentricities, and
contrariness were, yes, consistently infuriat-
ing and constant, but also inspiring. When I
told her she was starring in a whole chapter
of this book, she just shrugged. "It's the story
of my life." Modesty, according to Carol, is for
the birds.

Diving, Dumpster

Cuckoo Carol locked herself in the dumpster enclosure for a second time.

ME: Carol, I told you not to go in there!

CAROL: I'm looking for aluminum cans! People throw them in the wrong bin, you know.

ME: You can't go in there. Let me help you. . . .

CAROL: And I see a magazine I want. There's another one like it if you want it.

ME: I don't want trash! How long have you been stuck in there anyway?

CAROL: About an hour.

Out, Burned

One day, Carol followed our maintenance worker into the staff room. She was all the way back to the staff break room before he noticed her.

WORKER: What are you doing?! You can't come back here!

CAROL: Well! I thought you should know there's a light bulb out in the lobby!

WORKER: Will you please get out of here?

CAROL: [*After blowing a raspberry.*] Ungrateful!

Smart, Not

CAROL: The schedule on the wall says some group called FTPCU is using the meeting room tonight. What does FTPCU stand for?

ME: Hmm. I'm not sure. If they just use an acronym when they reserve the room, we don't know what group they are.

CAROL: Well, is there anyone here who's smarter than you?

Cubby, Returning to the

One day, I was working the reference desk when I turned to find Cuckoo Carol standing right next to me behind the counter.

ME: Carol! Why are you behind the desk?

CAROL: I was just returning the newspaper to the cubby hole.

ME: But you normally throw it down on the counter. What's different about today?

CAROL: Jeez Louise, I was *trying* to help. That's not anything you'd understand.

ME: Just leave it on the counter next time.

CAROL: Try to be more helpful next time! [*Sticks out her tongue.*]

Up, Mixing It

One day, Carol walked up to the desk with some items to return.

ME: Thank you! By the way, do you know about our return slot over there?

CAROL: Yes I do, but I don't like my things mixing with other people's things.

ME: Some people would argue that that's the point of a library.

CAROL: Don't get smart with me, young lady.

Dibs, Calling

CAROL: Is that a cane I see there in the lost and found? I've got dibs if no one comes back for it!

Trip, Bathroom

CAROL: I'm headed out to the bathroom.

ME: Okay, Carol.

CAROL: I'm supposed to drink a lot of water before I donate blood tomorrow. That's why I need the bathroom. Because of all the water. Because I'm donating blood. I need to use the bathroom!

Buffet, Library

There was a community group using our meeting room, and Carol walked in to get some of the refreshments.

PROGRAM ORGANIZER: [*somewhat bewildered*] Oh, are you here for the program?

CAROL: I always come if there's a buffet.

Drill, Just a

We had a fire drill at the library. Cuckoo Carol hates being out of the loop, so she's always the last to leave. Here was our mid-evacuation conversation:

CAROL: Is this just a drill or what?

ME: Please evacuate the building now.

CAROL: [*Slowly hobbling toward door.*] I'm a-goin, I'm a-goin'. I don't see any smoke though.

ME: Please just keep going. You're the last one!

CAROL: [*stopping*] What if I don't wanna?

ME: Exit the building. You're almost there!

CAROL: Don't be so pushy. My hip hurts, you know. If this is just a drill, I might have to see my lawyer about this. I don't know why you won't just tell me. I could help you, you know.

ME: Look, if you don't exit the library, we can't give the "all clear" and that means you can't use the computer today.

CAROL: If there was a real fire, I suppose you'd just leave me at the computer to burn up, wouldn't you?

ME: —

CAROL: I'm a-goin', I'm a-goin'.

That, Not All Like

I was shelving DVDs when Carol came to ask me for recommendations for television shows.

ME: Well, what types of things do you like to watch?

CAROL: Things about Mormons, but not those nasty shows that portray them as bamboozlers and polygons. We're not all like that, you know.

Betsys, Toms and

One Saturday afternoon I noticed that Carol was attempting to hand out some religious leaflets to people in the lobby.

ME: Carol! You can't do that! There's no soliciting in the library.

CAROL: Why the hell not? These Toms and Betsys need some Jesus in their lives and it's up to me to show them the way.

Diet, Balanced

One day I overheard Carol state this to another library patron:

CAROL: I eat two brownies and two chocolate milks a day and I haven't been sick in years.

Empty, Coming Up

While checking in returned items I noticed that Carol returned an empty DVD case, so I gave her a call and she answered her phone right away.

ME: Hello, Carol! It's Gina from the library. You forgot to put the DVD in the case you returned today.

CAROL: Oh, I don't think so.

ME: Well, I have the empty case here, if you could just check your player—

CAROL: Impossible!

ME: Would you please just check—

CAROL: I'd rather do two hundred million things than listen to you.

Day, Staff Training

The library was closed for our annual staff training day and most of the parking lot was roped off. As the maintenance crew set up chairs for our opening speaker, I noticed Carol's very distinct car slowly swerving around the cones and come to a sideways stop. As she started to get out of her car, I stepped forward to thwart her.

ME: Carol, we are closed today. We've had signs up all month and you just drove past the cones blocking off the parking spaces.

CAROL: I'll just go inside and get to work while you play your little games.

Choices, Making

One day a patron sat down at the table Carol usually occupied in the Quiet Room.

CAROL: This is ridiculous. Kindly go tell that woman she can't sit in my chair.

ME: It's not your chair. She's not doing anything wrong. Why don't you choose a different spot today?

CAROL: Why don't you pick a different attitude?

Sweet Sorrow, Parting Is Such

On my last day of work at that library branch, Carol approached me.

CAROL: I just want you to know that some people around here will probably miss you when you're gone.

ME: That's . . . very sweet of you. Will you miss me?

CAROL: Maybe so. But don't let it go to your head.

Chapter 9

611 Human Anatomy

When humans enter the library with fully functioning (or dysfunctioning) bodies, very human things happen—like farts and vomit and attempts at medical diagnoses and sexual inappropriateness. Being a librarian means that you sometimes have to take on other roles, like school nurse, first responder, and even sex therapist. Library school may cost an arm and a leg, but it doesn't equip us with this body of knowledge. We just do our best to deal with these situations, er, head on.

Tooth, Missing

A man was waiting in line by the front desk. I noticed him cough and then gag a little. He then spit something out of his mouth. A small tooth landed on the carpet.

MAN: [*Without blinking an eye, picks up the tooth, puts it in his pocket, and looks up.*] Can I get some help with the computer?

Master, Yoga

I was walking through the library and came upon a twenty-something man sitting in a cross-legged yoga pose on top of a table.

ME: Sir, you can't sit on top of the table.

MAN: *I have every right to sit here!*

Snakes, Don't Like

An elderly woman came in to the Youth Services department one afternoon to check out some Bible stories for her Sunday school when she noticed the model rattlesnake on top of our cabinet.

LADY: Is that a snake?!

ME: Yes, but it's just made out of brown paper.

LADY: Good. I don't like snakes. Not because they're slimy, but because they're not. They feel muscular [*whispers*] like a man's penis.

Crack, Reference Room

A woman approached me at the desk.

WOMAN: I want to show you this photo I took in the reference room just now, but I don't want you to think I'm a weirdo.

ME: [*Leaning over and looking at her phone and at what appeared to be a zoomed-in photo of a male patron's bare backside.*] Did he moon you?!

WOMAN: No, he just had plumber's crack. Big time, wouldn't you say? Anyway, I didn't want to have to be the one to tell him. I'm erasing this picture right now. You see me erasing it, right? I'm not a pervert!

Doctor, I'm Not a

PATRON: I need to come around and show you something.

ME: [*Slow on the uptake.*] Hmm?

PATRON: [*Comes behind reference desk and removes shoe.*]

ME: Um, you—

PATRON: See how my foot is swollen? I need to Google it to see what's wrong with it but I don't know what to Google. Would you say it's inflamed or irritated?

ME: I'm sorry, I really can't give medical advice.

PATRON: I just need to know what to Google.

Math, Marijuana Versus

A gentleman reeking of marijuana approached me at the desk.

MAN: Excuse me, there were some math books checked out on my card, like, two years ago, but I don't even like math! Can you do anything about it, dude?

Ass, Yiddish for

A woman drove twenty-five miles to the library one day to determine whether our meeting room chairs were comfortable enough for a two-hour meeting she was planning to attend in a few months.

WOMAN: I have a sensitive *tuches*. That's Yiddish for "ass."

Cheese, Avoid the

A woman wearing a sterile mask over her nose and mouth came into the library. There were hot pink lips drawn onto the front of the mask in lipstick. She picked up the key to the bathroom and then stopped to ask me a question when another patron inquired about the key.

WOMAN IN MASK: Oh, honey, you can take it, but hurry. Hurry. I need to keep it near. I had some cheese for lunch and it is killing me. *Killing me!*

WOMAN IN MASK: [*After returning from a half-hour trip to the bathroom and being approached by another patron inquiring about the key.*] Oh, but puh-lease bring it back straight to me. I had some pro-vo-lon-ee today, just two little pieces, but boy is it killing me. Don't ever eat pro-vo-lon-ee if you can help it. *Please hurry and bring the key back!*

Let Go, Learning to

One day, a library clerk came upon a disgusting sight—in the stacks was a sweatshirt that was obviously soiled with vomit. Horrified, she came to me for help. I put on some rubber gloves, carefully picked up the wet, nasty thing, and placed it into a plastic bag that went straight to the dumpster. Then I scoured the metal shelving and disinfected.

Incredibly, later that day, a man called to claim it.

ME: But sir, did you throw up on your sweatshirt?

MAN: Yes, I think it was food poisoning. It was awful!

ME: Yes, it was! It was not a very nice thing to find on our shelf. I threw it away.

MAN: No! Did you really just throw it away?

ME: Let me see if I'm hearing you right. You came to the library, threw up on yourself, left the shirt for someone else to find, and now you are calling to claim it?

MAN: Um, yes.

ME: You do realize this sounds a bit strange, right?

MAN: I'm sorry I got sick. Am I allowed to come back to the library?

ME: Uh, sure, just don't throw up, okay?

Drugs, Good

ME: Good morning!

PATRON: It's always nice to see your smiling face. You must be on the good drugs.

ME: —

Guy, Crutch

I recently waited on an older, well-dressed gentleman who mentioned seeing someone using crutches outside the library.

CRUTCH GUY: Did you ever have to use crutches?

ME: Yes, years ago.

CRUTCH GUY: What happened? How old were you? Did it hurt? Did you know right away there was a break? How long did you need to use the crutches? Was your foot in a cast or a brace? How did it feel?

I answered his questions one by one, thinking to myself, *This is sort of strange small talk,* when I noticed that his breathing was quickening and his face was flushed. I quickly made an excuse and sent him on his way. Afterwards, I told a coworker about the exchange.

COWORKER: [*Whispering to another coworker.*] Psst, crutch guy was in!

Odors, Computer Lab

A woman came to the desk with a complaint:

WOMAN: There is a man in the computer lab who smells like Swiss cheese and crab cakes.

Idiot, I'm an

Early one morning, a man came into the library and asked to use our restroom. I quickly noticed that something was amiss about his facial hair.

MAN: [*Noticing my peculiar glance.*] Look, I was messing around this morning and shaved off half my mustache and I forgot to shave the rest before I left! Yes, I'm an idiot.

Books, Bored

One day, I heard a bit of a commotion in the children's area. I rushed over to find a mother of two scolding her seven-year-old son.

ME: What happened? Is everyone okay?

MOTHER: [*pointing at her baby*] Look!

The happy baby in the stroller had the word "BOOK" crudely written in green across her forehead, while the seven-year-old brother sat nearby holding an uncapped marker.

MOTHER: [*to her son*] Why did you do that?! You aren't supposed to draw on your sister!

SEVEN-YEAR-OLD: We were playing library!

Fungus, Types of

A woman came into the computer lab to get her husband. He signed off of the computer he was using and the two conversed on their way out the door.

WOMAN: Did you figure out what it was?

MAN: Yep. Google says I've got some kind of fingernail fungus. I promptly sanitized all of the computer keyboards in the room.

Chapter 10

621.385 Telephones

From fax machines to pay phones to smart-phones, one of the greatest innovations can sometimes be the greatest source of hilarity, especially in a library. Because there really is a fine line between use, misuse, and abuse when it comes to the telephone, whether the patrons are calling each other or us. Grab some soup cans and string, phone a friend, or call for help because this chapter covers the disconnect everyone experiences when the phone starts to ring in the stacks.

Connections, Faxy

I just tried to fax something for a patron. The number she gave me rang and then a person on the other end answered loudly enough for the whole library to hear:

PERSON: [*answering phone call*] "You've reached Sexy Connections! Meet your soulmate or just a good time!

Woes, Mobile

After asking a man in the quiet room to please end his phone call, he became quite upset and tried to reason with me.

MAN: It's not my fault that people call me! If it's a number I don't recognize, I have to answer it in order to tell them not to call me. What would people think if I didn't answer my own phone?!

Shush Me, Can't

ME: I'm sorry ma'am, you'll have to take your cell phone call out to the lobby please.

WOMAN: [*in an exasperated voice*] But I'm talking to another library!

Rich, Too Damn

ME: [*answering telephone*] Thank you for calling the library, how may I help you?

FEMALE CALLER: They say I need a beginning reading teacher.

ME: A beginning reading teacher?

FEMALE CALLER: I know my reading! I've read all the classics. But I need my GED. I'm real good in reading, and I know my math. I know that half of six million is three million, and if you have that much money, you're too damn rich! I know if you take five dollars and split that in half, you and your friend can still get a soda pop. I need a GED tutor.

ME: I'm happy to transfer you to our Lifelong Learning Center!

M, Rated

After telling a twelve-year-old boy that he was too young to check out a rated M for Mature video game, he asked to borrow the phone to call his mother.

BOY: Mom? Yeah, I'm at the library right now. I need your permission to check out a rated M video game. [*pause*] The *M* stands for manly and that's basically what I am.

Voice, Having a Phone

We have a patron who calls at least once per day to brusquely ask several involved reference questions. I had heard stories about her and was dreading answering her call since I was new. When I finally got her, I answered all of her questions quickly and correctly.

PATRON: Thank you so much. You are quite helpful.

ME: [*relieved*] Well, thank you.

PATRON: But you really don't have a phone voice, so I wouldn't answer the phones anymore if I were you.

Signals, Crossed

ME: Thanks for calling the library, may I help you?

WOMAN: Yes, were you closed yesterday?

ME: No, we were open nine A.M. to five P.M. yesterday.

WOMAN: So you weren't closed?

ME: No.

WOMAN: Someone told me you were closed.

ME: Well, we weren't closed.

WOMAN: I wanted to make a computer reservation yesterday.

ME: Okay. Did you want to make a reservation today instead?

WOMAN: No thanks, I'm busy today. [*Click.*]

Typewriter, Needing a

ME: Thanks for calling the library, may I help you?

MAN: Do you have a typewriter there for public use?

ME: No I'm sorry, we don't, but I could tell you which libraries do ha—

MAN: But they don't *work*.

ME: Excuse me?

MAN: I've been to three other libraries and the typewriters are just junk! They don't *have* correction tape and I *need* that. Everyone needs that!

ME: —

MAN: You should have a typewriter. I mean, where are you supposed to go for a typewriter? It's pretty ridiculous, you know.

ME: We do have computers if that would—

MAN: No, no, no! *No* computers. A *typewriter*. With *correction tape*. I think someone should know about this. Who's in charge?

ME: Of the typewriters?

MAN: *Of everything!*

Threats, Death

ME: [*answering the phone*] Thanks for calling the library, may I help you?

MAN: I have reason to believe that someone at one of your public computers is sending me death threats.

ME: [*very concerned*] Have you called the police?

MAN: No. Maybe you could just tell him to stop?

ME: What does this person look like?

MAN: He's wearing a green shirt and blue jeans.

ME: Sir, you should call the police if you really feel like your life is in danger and they can investigate. There are privacy issues that I have to abide by, but a police officer could do more.

MAN: Oh, never mind. He just sent me a text saying he's sorry.

ME: Are you sure you don't want to call the police?

MAN: No. But can I make a computer reservation please?

Item, Lost

A patron called the library looking for an item in the lost and found.

PATRON: I think I left my computer charger in the library last night.

ME: I can check the lost and found. Can you describe the charger?

PATRON: It's black and has a cord that plugs into the wall.

Number, Call

A man came to the desk to inquire about a nonfiction book that was not in its place on the shelf.

MAN: I don't remember the name or author, but I wrote down the number location.

ME: Oh, okay, what was that call number?

MAN: [*Rattles off telephone number.*] Are you going to call me when you find it?

Slower, Go

ME: [*answering the telephone*] Thank you for calling the library. How may I help you?

MAN: Can you read me a list of all the books by John Grisham?

ME: Sure, I can help you with that. Are you looking for print books, audio, adult, young adult, youth fiction, nonfiction?

MAN: Just read me the list of his books.

ME: Okay. [*I start going through the list.*]

MAN: Can you go a little slower?

ME: Okay. Sure. [*I slow down.*]

About halfway through the list I notice a distinct change in the man's breathing.

ME: Are you okay, sir?

MAN: [*whispering, panting*] Oh, yeah, you like that don't you?

ME: [*Realizing what the man is most likely doing on the other end of the line.*] That's all the books by Grisham. Goodbye.

MAN: But I'm not done!

ME: I am!

Librarian, Shushing the

I was waiting on a gentleman when his mobile phone began to ring. He ignored its distinct ringtone and kept right on talking to me until it finally stopped.

MAN: You know, you might not want to carry your phone at work. It's rude.

ME: [*smiling*] Sir, I think the phone that was ringing is in your pocket.

MAN: [*immediately embarrassed, and apologetic*] I rarely carry a phone because it's so annoying.

ME: [*after laughing with the man*] It might be fun to tell people that you shushed a librarian today!

Weekend, Busy

During a particularly busy time, a woman phoned the library to ask about the running times of several films that were currently in theaters.

ME: I'm happy to look that information up for you, but would you mind terribly if I called you back? I have a line of people in front of me.

WOMAN: Sure, dearheart, I just need to know if I'll have time for all my suitors this weekend.

Dope, It Was

One afternoon while I was shelving, I overheard a man on his phone.

MAN: Yo, I don't know if it was real or not, but that scene in my head was dope. Did you see the dog spitting fire rainbows? I didn't think so, but it was dope!

Calls, Automaton

ME: Okay, I've requested the book for you. We'll call you with an automated message when it comes in.

WOMAN: Could you do my cell phone?

ME: Sure.

WOMAN: Is it like a text message?

ME: No, it'll be a voice message.

WOMAN: So you'll call me?

ME: Yes, it's an automated message telling you your book is here.

WOMAN: So it's an automaton? Or a robot calling?

ME: Sort of. A machine will leave you a message.

WOMAN: But how will I know it's from the library?

ME: That's what the message will say!

WOMAN: Is it a text message?

ME: . . . are you joking?

WOMAN: I think I get it. I just have to wait, right?

Chapter 11

808.879083 Children's Humor

Kids can be pretty tough on books. They wipe boogers on pages, gnaw on the corners, and spill food and liquids on the covers. But nothing makes me happier than to see a child rush out of story time and into the library, on a quest for the perfect book about dogs or science or jokes or underwear-clad superheroes. Cheers to the parents and teachers who bring kids to the library, for they provide endless entertainment to the librarians. Grab a carpet square and sidle up to the front row, because children's story time is about to begin.

Guesses, Two More

Overheard in the children's library:

FOUR-YEAR-OLD: Mama, could we get *Frumpystiltskin*?

Individuality, Enthusiastic

ME: Hello and welcome to our garden program. Let's go around the circle and everyone say their name and their favorite fruit or vegetable!

CHILD 1: I'm Abby. I like tomatoes.

CHILD 2: I'm George. I like peppers.

CHILD 3: I'm David. I'm weird!

Applicant, The

On a seventh grader's application to volunteer at the library: "My many years of schooling have prepared me to be a good public speaker, plus I work well with kids that can walk."

Worker, Girl

I was walking through the children's section where a four-year-old boy was sitting by himself at a table.

BOY: Hi! Are you the girl worker?

ME: I am! Are you having a nice time?

BOY: Yes, I am. I really like this little book here. [*Holds up book.*]

ME: Good! You can take it home with you if your mom or dad lets you.

BOY: See that girl over there with the white T-shirt? She's my grandma.

ME: Oh, okay. Well, have fun!

BOY: Bye! I like your books!

Prizes, All of the

A six-year-old kid wandered up to the Summer Reading Club table and announced:

KID: I will win *all of the prizes*! I am a reader! I am a megasaurus reader. *Rawr! [Puts a book on his head and runs away.]*

Skills, Important

FOUR-YEAR-OLD GIRL: Mommy, I'm only going to school until I learn to read and write. Then I can take care of myself.

Books, Library

KID: Does this computer have games?

ME: That's a catalog computer. You use it to look up books the library has.

KID: Where are the books?

ME: Look around you!

KID: *[Turns away from the computer, notices the rows and rows of books, gasps in awe.]*

Ouchies, Library

I stubbed my toe just as someone dropped a book into the inside book drop. As I yelped and howled in pain, a child on the other side said:

CHILD: Mommy, I think we hurt the book!

Aardvarks, Raising

SIX-YEAR-OLD GIRL: Do you have books about aardvarks? I want one for a pet, but my mother doesn't think it's a very good idea.

Reports, State

A little boy was wandering around the nonfiction section.

ME: Can I help you?

BOY: I need to write a report on New Hampster and I can't find anything!

Imagination, Using Your

As I was walking through the children's area, I noticed a toddler sitting on a chair at the end of a bookshelf. He had bare legs and his pants were around his ankles. I walked up to him and he smiled cherubically.

ME: What are you doing?

BOY: Pretending to go poop.

Job, Good

Five-year-old girl, as her mom put some items in the book return:

GIRL: Good job, Mommy! You're doing a very good job! One at a time, please, one at a time.

Murder, Liking

I always ask my book group to rate the books we read on a scale of one to five, five being the highest rating. Tonight was the works of Edgar Allan Poe.

TEEN GIRL 1: I'd only give it a four because I don't really like murder and dismemberment.

TEEN GIRL 2: I'd give it a five because I actually *do* like murder and dismemberment.

Lady, Library

ANGRY TEN-YEAR-OLD TO HIS MOM: I hope you're happy! I've had to look at books for *hours* while you were gone. The library lady said this is no daycare! Do I look like a baby?!

Too Much Information, No Such Thing as

ME: [*To four-year-old girl.*] Hi there, kiddo! What're you up to today?

FOUR-YEAR-OLD: Today is Daddy day! We had breakfast and came to the library! Daddy said Mama needs a break. Daddy starts with the letter D and I still nurse my mama. Daddy says they're trying to weeeeeeeeeean me, but I'm too smart!

Envy, Librarian

At story time, three little girls who stood in the front row shared their thoughts with the children's librarian.

GIRL 1: I like your shoes.

GIRL 2: I wish I had your finger puppets.

GIRL 3: I want to be you.

Cars, Before

YOUNG GIRL: [*After I showed her an old wooden card catalog.*] Is this what they had before there were cars?

Orphans, Library

I was helping Avery, a six-year-old library regular, at the children's reference desk when I overheard the next kid in line talking to his mother.

KID: [*Whispering, pointing at Avery.*] Mom, why is that girl here alone?

MOM: I'm sure her parents are nearby. Don't worry about it.

KID: [*Shouting, as I turned to walk Avery to the stacks.*] ARE YOU AN ORPHAN?

Questions, Profound

I was at the children's reference desk when a boy of about six approached me, nervously huffing and stuttering.

KID: Um . . . uh . . . d-d-d-d-d-do you . . . um . . . are you. . . .

ME: [*Hanging on his every syllable, waiting for a profound kid question like: "Where are the Goosebumps books?" or "Do you have Captain Underpants?"*]

KID: I-I-I-am . . . wo-wo-wondering . . . if-if-if-if-if you will have. . . .

ME: [*Thinking to myself, Maybe he needs help! Or maybe he has some great reference question that only a boy of this caliber of specialness could ask—spit it out, kid!*]

KID: Are . . . are . . . are you going to have penguins in the library tomorrow?

ME: —

KID: W-W-W-Well?

ME: Um, no. Sadly, we will not have penguins in the library tomorrow. But I wish we would!

KID: [*Smiles and walks away.*]

Cinnamons, Crime

One morning, one of my favorite five-year-olds tromped up to the desk.

FIVE-YEAR-OLD: Hello! Where are your books on crooks?

ME: Crooks?

FIVE-YEAR-OLD: You know, scoundrels and mobsters.

MOTHER: [*chiming in*] We had a long visit from grandpa this weekend.

FIVE-YEAR-OLD: You got books on Al Capone? He led a crime cinnamon.

MOTHER: Syndicate.

Snowman, Purple

Overheard in the children's library:

CHILD: I'm gonna color my snowman purple. I bet he gets tired of being white.

Sister, Kid

A little boy wandered up to the desk with a Franny K. Stein book.

BOY: I'm reading this to my sister 'cause she can't read yet. It's not her fault, she's too little. Mom says I'm a very nice brother, but [*looks around, whispers*] I actually like this book a lot. Don't tell her I said so 'cause she gives me ice cream when she thinks I'm being real nice.

Chapter 12

809.9339 Volumes of Gratitude

I could never even think that being a librarian is a thankless job. Amid the humor and colorful characters, there are some wonderfully touching things going on in libraries every day. Being moved to tears on a regular basis is one of the perks of the job, especially when the tears aren't from cat dander or book dust. From Doughnut Guy to Library Princesses, these stories blur my vision and warm my heart. This is what working at a public library is all about.

Grow Up, When I

I was working at the interior book drop when I overheard a young girl and her mother on the other side of the wall.

GIRL: [*In a tiny voice.*] Mommy, do you know what I want to be when I grow up?

MOMMY: No. What?

GIRL: I want to be a sparkle librarian.

MOMMY: What do you mean?

GIRL: Like the librarian who reads us stories. She's always smiling and wears nice jewelry!

Thanks, Giving

Around noon, a man I didn't recognize came into the library with several huge platters of food from a local restaurant.

MAN: I thought I'd cater your staff's lunch today! [*Places platters on the counter.*] You all helped me apply for a job last year when I was at my lowest. Well, I got the job and never forgot it. I wanted to do something for you.

ME: [*Thanking him with tears in my eyes, and then he quickly leaves.*]

Cool, Kinda

BOY: Thanks for the books. Hey, you know something?

ME: What's that?

BOY: You're kinda cool.

Books, Smaller

I once helped a family new to the United States get library cards. After giving them an overview about the library, I showed the kids the children's area. The mother told them they could each check out two books. The smallest child, a girl of seven, picked out two small board books meant for babies.

ME: Are you sure you don't want a picture book? [*Shows her a few new titles that are on display.*]

GIRL: Too much money.

ME: What do you mean?

GIRL: These cost less, right? Smaller.

ME: [*After realizing that she was trying to save her parents' money by choosing the smallest books.*] Do you know what? All of this is free, no money. You can choose whichever books you want.

She turned her head to look at the shelves and shelves of books and quietly gasped. She wandered away without another word, and I watched her pick up book after book—shuffling through each one, making little piles, and studying each one intently—caught up in the wonder of the bounty.

Lives, Saving

I was in my office when one of the library assistants came to my desk in tears.

ME: What's wrong?

ASSISTANT: [*sobbing*] I'm overcome with kindness!

After she sat down and wiped her eyes, her story came out.

A man she had helped at the computers a few days before came in to thank her. He is a non-native English speaker who had been having trouble accessing his new employer's website in order to fill out some information needed to complete the hiring process.

MAN: If I do not fill in correctly by end of day, they might take job offer away from me. That can't happen. I've worked so hard to get job. I have family—

ASSISTANT: [*sitting down beside him*] I will help you.

After trying and failing to save the information they'd spent several minutes inputting, the library assistant recognized that the website was not working properly. Instead of giving up, she found the contact information for the webmaster and spent several minutes trying to explain the rather complicated situation to that person by online chat and then telephone. In the end, the webmaster made a correction to the code and they were finally able to save and submit the information required by the company to secure our patron's employment.

ME: This is wonderful! You did a great job!

ASSISTANT: That's not all. The man and his entire family are outside your office waiting to tell you how great I am.

I went out into the library and met the man. He was beaming, and so was his wife, mother, son, daughter, brother, and sister-in-law. We all shook hands and thanked each other.

MAN: I will tell everyone I know to come here. This place saves lives.

Love, Library

A young boy came into the library.

BOY: [*with an enthusiastic outside voice*] *I love the library!*

ME: I'm glad you love the library!

BOY: We come here every Wednesday. I'm gonna come in here every Wednesday until the day I die.

Toes, Keeping Them on Their

We held a *Super Smash Bros. Brawl* video game tournament for teenagers at the library. Thirty kids showed up. The only girl in attendance won.

ME: That's awesome! So did you practice a whole lot or do you just play all the time?

GIRL: I like the game, but sometimes you just gotta keep boys on their toes. [*Turns and leaves.*]

Signing, Book

We had a regular patron who would often come in to our library to check out audiobooks. He suffered from a neurological disorder and was a quadriplegic. One day, a woman called and said our patron had self-published an autobiography and he wanted to know if he could hold a book signing at our library. For several reasons, we do not normally work directly with self-published authors, but I talked my boss into making an exception this time. I'm glad I did.

It turned out to be one of our library's most popular events. Over 200 people came to the signing, including the mayor and local celebrities. Dozens of copies of the man's book sold and the proceeds went to a fund for his medical care.

Sadly, less than a year later, the man passed away. He was only in his late twenties, but he lived a full life. Besides writing a book, he attained a college degree despite the adversity he faced. Staff and patrons often speak fondly of him and we still have his book on our shelf.

One of the best things about being a librarian is working at the intersection of life and the written word. This man's personal story didn't contain volumes, but his was an epic journey. He helped me to see that every page matters and each character we encounter helps to shape who we are and how we choose to live.

Pacing, Pay Phone

Years ago when there was a pay phone at the library, a man we'd never seen before started coming into the branch every day for several hours at a time. From the time we opened until about noon, he would pace back and forth in front of the pay phone in the lobby, tossing a quarter up in the air. Back and forth he would walk as if waiting for the phone to ring. One day, after a couple of weeks of the same routine, those of us who worked the reference desk were surprised to hear the pay phone ring. The man answered it and excitedly spoke into the receiver. After the call, he walked up to the desk, elated, and shared with us his story.

MAN: I lost my job about a month ago and I just couldn't bear to tell my wife. I've been leaving the house each morning, searching for work. Each afternoon I've been applying for jobs and going on interviews, and each morning I've waited here by the phone because that's the number I gave out to prospective employers. Well, today I got the call! I got a job!

Guy, Doughnut

You know those television shows where someone throws a dart at a map and travels to the town they hit and randomly chooses someone from the phone book and finds something remarkable about that person and does a story about them? I had an experience like that, but the remarkable person just wandered into my library looking for doughnuts.

Let me back up.

An older man walked up to me at the reference desk and asked for the location of the nearest Krispy Kreme Doughnuts.

MAN: See, I'm eighty-three years old and I thought it was time for a Krispy Kreme doughnut.

ME: Good idea! [*I type "Krispy Kreme" into a search engine.*] Oh. It looks like the closest store is one hundred thirty-four miles away.

MAN: [*dejected*] Is that right! I was willing to drive a little ways, but. . . .

ME: Sometimes they sell them at grocery stores and gas stations. Let's check!

I did another search to no avail, and when I called the corporate number, I was informed that stores that carried them were even farther away.

MAN: [*looking miserable*] Well, thanks for trying.

ME: [*Because I hate not giving people the answers they want.*] Lucky for you, I'm going to Los Angeles this weekend and they're bound to have some there. Tell you what, call me on Monday morning at nine and ask me if I have some doughnuts for you.

MAN: [*excited*] I couldn't ask you to do that!

ME: But you didn't ask. Plus, you're eighty-three!

I wrote down my name and the library's telephone number for him.

At the end of a marvelous trip, I stopped at the Krispy Kreme store in Burbank and ordered a dozen glazed doughnuts and some chocolate ones for me.

Sure enough, on Monday morning, the man called.

ME: [*happily*] I have a dozen little somethings for you!

When he arrived, he was incredibly grateful and pulled out a neat stack of money—not a wad, a stack—and offered to pay. But I had a plan to avoid an awkward money exchange.

ME: I won't accept money, but if you would tell me one interesting story about your life, over a doughnut, [*licking my lips*] you'll be off the hook.

So we broke all the rules and started eating doughnuts in the library as he told his story.

Bob was the editor for his steel company's magazine in the 1950s when the Cold War was brewing. The United States government decided to send eleven people to Russia as a sort of cultural exchange (read: to spy on them). They sent an athlete, a businessman, and some others, and decided to ask one magazine editor—Bob was nominated. Not only was he an award-winning editor, but he was also a freelance photographer who'd won all sorts of awards. He was in Russia for six months and took 3,000 color shots of everything he could get his sights on, including the Kremlin, sometimes hiding his camera in his jacket and coughing to cover the sound of the shutter. When he got back to the United States, the government took possession of 250 of the photos. He made a documentary film about his experience, won several civilian awards, and was asked to speak and show his film all over the country.

ME: You're a *spy!*

MAN: Oh, I'm just a dying man who wanted a doughnut.

ME: Well, now you've got eleven. Now get out of here and save the world.

MAN: Call me if there's anything I can ever do for you, you hear? [*Turns to my coworker.*] Isn't she remarkable?

Index

About the Author

Gina Sheridan holds a BA in English Literature, Society, and Politics from Webster University and a Master of Library and Information Studies from the University of Alabama. Her interests include YA fiction, social media, cemeteries, entertaining, urban exploration, and book art. She lives in Old North St. Louis with her husband and cats. She can be found online at *ginasheridan.com*.